GUIDE DOGS

By Sara Green

BELLWETHER M........EAPOLIS, MN

Jump into the cockpit and take flight with Pilot books. Your journey will take you on high-energy adventures as you learn about all that is wild, weird, fascinating, and fun!

This edition first published in 2014 by Bellwether Media, Inc.

No part of this publication may be reproduced in whole or in part without written permission of the publisher. For information regarding permission, write to Bellwether Media, Inc., Attention: Permissions Department, 5357 Penn Avenue South, Minneapolis, MN 55419.

Library of Congress Cataloging-in-Publication Data

Green, Sara, 1964-
Guide dogs / by Sara Green.
    pages cm. – (Pilot: Dogs to the rescue!)
Includes bibliographical references and index.
Summary: "Engaging images accompany information about guide dogs. The combination of high-interest subject matter and narrative text is intended for students in grades 3 through 7"–Provided by publisher.
ISBN 978-1-60014-955-9 (hardcover : alk. paper)
1. Guide dogs–Juvenile literature. I. Title.
HV1780.G74 2014
362.4'183–dc23

2013004877

Printed in the United States of America, North Mankato, MN.

TABLE OF CONTENTS

A GUIDE DOG HERO

On September 11, 2001, Michael Hingson was working at his desk on the seventy-eighth floor of the World Trade Center. His guide dog Roselle slept quietly at his feet. Suddenly, Michael heard an explosion. A plane had crashed into the building!

The noise woke Roselle. She waited for Michael to give her instructions. Michael smelled smoke and heard people shouting. He stood up and grabbed Roselle's **harness**. "Forward," he said. Roselle guided Michael to a stairwell. The stairwell was dark and smoky, but Roselle remained calm. She guided Michael and others down more than 1,000 stairs. They reached fresh air and safety moments before the building collapsed. Roselle helped save many lives that day.

5

WHAT ARE GUIDE DOGS?

Golden
Retriever

Specially trained canines called guide dogs make sure sight challenges do not prevent their **handlers** from being **mobile**. They lead people who are blind or **visually impaired** from one place to another. Walking outdoors and in public places is easier with a guide dog. The dog can see the safest route and guide the handler away from obstacles. Public places, including schools, restaurants, and malls, welcome guide dogs. Buses, trains, subways, and airplanes let guide dogs ride along with their handlers.

Guide dogs must be intelligent, friendly, and alert. They must enjoy serving people. They also must have **stamina** to work long days. The most common guide dog breeds are Labrador Retrievers, Golden Retrievers, and German Shepherds. Some people also use Standard Poodles or Boxers as guide dogs.

Breeds of Guide Dogs

Labrador Retriever

German Shepherd

Standard Poodle

Boxer

Puppy raisers take care of guide dogs when the dogs are young. These volunteers provide loving homes and give the young dogs a lot of attention. Puppies are placed with their raisers when they are about 8 weeks old. The raisers teach the puppies basic obedience skills. They also introduce the dogs to many different people, settings, and sounds to socialize them. Raisers take the puppies to grocery stores, schools, restaurants, and malls. Many puppies ride on airplanes with their raisers. These experiences help the puppies grow up to be confident, calm, and trustworthy guide dogs.

Profile: Labrador Retriever

Intelligence

The Lab is the seventh smartest dog breed. It will learn new commands with little repetition and will obey them almost every time.

Size

Height: 21 to 25 inches (53 to 64 centimeters)

Weight: 60 to 90 pounds (27 to 41 kilograms)

Characteristics

The Lab is full of energy. This allows the dog to work long days. The breed is also loyal, which makes it a perfect service companion.

GUIDE DOGS IN TRAINING

After around one year of living with puppy raisers, the dogs are sent to a special guide dog school. Here, they receive advanced training from professional dog trainers. Training usually lasts four to five months. Guide dog trainers always use **positive reinforcement**. They give a lot of praise to encourage good work. Food rewards are not used often. Guide dogs must be able to work around food without being distracted by it.

The first step is learning how to walk with handlers. Guide dogs walk just ahead and to the left of their handlers. They must walk in a straight line and keep a steady pace. Guide dogs have to learn to ignore other animals, people, and food. This helps them stay focused on their handlers. Guide dogs also learn to find specific objects on command. They can guide handlers to elevator buttons, trash cans, soda machines, and places to sit.

Guide dogs must also learn how to cross streets in traffic. When a guide dog reaches a curb, it stops. This signals to its handler that they have reached a crosswalk. The dog is not trained to read traffic lights. Instead, the handler listens to the flow of traffic to decide when it is safe to cross.

First American Guide Dog

In 1928, Morris Frank became the first American to use a guide dog. His dog was a German Shepherd named Buddy. In 1929, Frank started a guide dog school called The Seeing Eye. Today, the school matches about 260 people and guide dogs every year.

When the handler hears that traffic has stopped, he or she gives a forward command. If the dog sees no danger, it guides the handler across the street. However, it disobeys the command and refuses to move if it sees or hears something its handler missed. This practice, called **intelligent disobedience**, has saved many lives.

A PERFECT MATCH

Once the dogs have completed their training, they are matched with handlers. The guide dog schools match handlers and dogs based on the dog's **temperament** and the handler's lifestyle. The teams spend up to a month at the school working with the dog trainers. The guide dogs and handlers soon develop deep bonds of trust.

The trainers teach handlers everything they need to know about working with a guide dog. Handlers learn all the commands the dogs know and how to walk with the dogs. At the same time, the guide dogs learn to obey the handlers instead of the trainers. Soon, they can understand each other's movements. A graduation ceremony marks the end of training. The puppy raisers are invited to attend. They help the handlers, dog trainers, and guide dogs celebrate their achievements. Now the handlers and guide dogs are ready to act as a true team!

ON AND OFF THE JOB

Guide dogs wear a special harness when they work. The dogs often wag their tails when they see the harness. They understand that this is their uniform. When it is on, they know it is time to work! The harness also lets people in public recognize that guide dogs are on the job. People should not talk to or pet guide dogs wearing harnesses. The dogs need to stay focused on their handlers.

Guide dogs at work do not play, bark, or seek attention from strangers or other animals. The dogs only walk with their handlers. When their handlers sit, the dogs rest quietly at their feet. However, when the harness comes off, the dogs are free to play and act like any other pet.

harness

Quick Learners

Many guide dogs quickly learn all of their handler's usual destinations. When handlers tell their dogs to go to school or the office, the dogs know exactly where to go without directions.

Guide dogs work as long as they are in excellent physical and mental shape. They usually **retire** just before they enter old age. Older dogs are often sharp enough to keep working, but they may slow down. They may not be able to keep up with their handlers. Guide dogs usually retire when they are around 10 years old. But some work for a little longer. Some guide dogs can work until age 13!

When a guide dog retires, it goes to a loving home. Often, the handler chooses to keep the dog as a pet. Sometimes guide dogs return to their original puppy raisers. Guide dog schools usually have a waiting list of people who want to adopt a retired guide dog. The people hope for an intelligent, friendly dog with great manners! Retired guide dogs are honored and loved as wonderful friends no matter where they live.

HIKING WITH ORIENT

In 1990, a German Shepherd named Orient helped his handler, Bill Irwin, hike the Appalachian Trail. Orient even carried his own food in a dog backpack! The Appalachian Trail is a challenging hiking trail. It winds through forests and national parks as it makes its way across 14 states. Irwin and Orient completed the almost 2,200-mile (3,500-kilometer) trail in just over eight months.

The Appalachian Trail

Maine

N
W · E
S

Atlantic Ocean

Georgia

Quite a Hike
Orient and Irwin hiked from Georgia to Maine without a map, GPS device, or compass!

Orient was Irwin's eyes and helped him navigate obstacles along the way. These obstacles included large rocks, cliffs, and streams. He kept a slow pace and stopped at the obstacles. Orient even learned to identify and follow trail markers. When the pair got lost, Orient could pick up the scent of other hikers to get back to the trail. With Orient's help, Irwin became the first blind person to hike the entire Appalachian Trail without other people!

GLOSSARY

handlers—people who are responsible for highly trained dogs

harness—a strap that fits around a dog's shoulders and chest

intelligent disobedience—when a guide dog refuses to follow a command in order to keep the handler safe from harm

mobile—able to move around with ease

obedience skills—skills that include sit, stay, come, and down

positive reinforcement—using rewards to praise good behavior

puppy raisers—volunteers who care for puppies that will grow up to be guide dogs and service dogs

retire—to stop working

socialize—to teach dogs to have good manners in all kinds of situations

stamina—the ability to do something for a long time

temperament—personality or nature

visually impaired—having limited vision

volunteers—people who do something to be kind rather than for money or another reward

TO LEARN MORE

AT THE LIBRARY

Bozzo, Linda. *Guide Dog Heroes*. Berkeley Heights, N.J.: Enslow Publishers, 2011.

Hall, Becky. *Morris and Buddy: The Story of the First Seeing Eye Dog*. Morton Grove, Ill.: Albert Whitman & Co., 2007.

McDaniel, Melissa. *Guide Dogs*. New York, N.Y.: Bearport, 2005.

ON THE WEB

Learning more about guide dogs is as easy as 1, 2, 3.

1. Go to www.factsurfer.com.

2. Enter "guide dogs" into the search box.

3. Click the "Surf" button and you will see a list of related Web sites.

With factsurfer.com, finding more information is just a click away.

INDEX